THE ROYAL AIR FORCE
IN COLOUR

Right:
Tornado team: pilot and navigator stand in front of their Tornado all-weather fighter of No 229 OCU.

Above:
Self portrait — the author (standing) and Flt Lt Spike Newbery with Hawk T1A pod camera ship XX317. The Rolleiflex camera is mounted in the Carrier Bomb Light Store (CBLS) under the port wing.

CHRIS ALLAN
AIR FORCE
IN COLOUR

LONDON
IAN ALLAN LTD

CONTENTS

Acknowledgements

To the RAF for the opportunity, to Paul Jackson for his assistance, and to many, many others . . . *Thank you*

First published 1988

ISBN 0 7110 1725 5

Published by Ian Allan Ltd, Shepperton, Surrey; and printed by Ian Allan Printing Ltd at their works at Coombelands in Runnymede, England

Above:
Although Harrier squadrons are assigned to and located on conventional airfields in peacetime, they periodically deploy to dispersed sites, their operational environment in time of war. After coming to cockpit readiness, this No 1 Squadron GR3 will be tasked for its next mission via telebrief.

DEFENCE OF THE REALM

MANY ARE CALLED BUT FEW ARE CHOSEN

St Matthew 22:14

Rare, indeed, are the clubs and societies with membership conditions stricter than those governing entry to the elite band known as Royal Air Force aircrew. Rigorous selection procedures and world-renowned training standards ensure that pilots entrusted with some of the West's foremost combat aircraft are second to none in their profession. Once awarded his coveted wings — worn proudly on the light blue RAF uniform — the newly-qualified pilot is at the threshold of a career in which he may fly a diversity of aircraft types from strike-fighter to docile trainer.

Many of these he will never have the opportunity to sample, but training exercises and visits to other airfields will soon familiarise him with aircraft flown by his compatriots. Uniquely, in these pages is such an inside view of the RAF, portraying events in the daily life of a serving officer. Furthermore, this *tour de* (air) *force* employs entirely original illustrations, each taken by the author, to depict all the significant types of aircraft in current service.

The pilot — particularly the student approaching the crossroads of his training — classifies aircraft differently from the strategist. The latter speaks of fighters, bombers, reconnaissance, transport and others according to their function, yet to the prospective RAF pilot, there are but three sub-divisions: Fast Jet, Multi-Engine and Helicopter. It is during training that a pilot's aptitude for one of these three avenues is assessed, and it is usual for at least the first part of his career to be spent possibly flying several types of aircraft within the specified category.

Accordingly, the ensuing chapters will reflect this aviator's view of aircraft types in slightly expanded form. Within such broad guide-lines, individual flying tasks are varied. 'Fast Jet' can mean the exhilaration of air-to-air combat or a breathtaking, low-level dash through strongly defended territory on a strike mission. 'Multi-Engine' (alternatively described as 'Slow Jet') could be hauling mixed freight and the licentious soldiery around the globe, or conducting HM Queen Elizabeth on a state visit. 'Helicopter' might involve airlifting an anti-aircraft missile battery across North Germany or plucking shipwrecked sailors from a heaving deck in atrocious weather.

The training machines which were the means to a squadron are not forgotten, because some pilots are chosen to transfer their skills to the next generation of fliers — as has been the case for the RAF's 'three score years and ten' of existence. With the normal 'tour' of service lasting approximately three years, an officer may expect at least one session instructing pre- or post-graduate pilots during his career, as well as a perhaps less-welcome term 'flying a mahogany bomber' (a ground tour on administrative duties).

Progressive disappearance of pink areas of the world's map since Queen Victoria's days have not entirely removed the opportunity for flying and serving overseas, for the red, white and blue roundel (with white omitted on tactical aircraft) is still borne aloft in far-off skies. Some of the pictures which follow were taken during training visits abroad: either to hone skills at weapons camps or liaise with allies. Britain's commitment to NATO is by far the principal reason for such activities, although outside Europe, territories such as Hong Kong, Belize and the Falkland Islands continue to host RAF aircraft.

Should the task in hand not warrant a full squadron — usually of between 12 and 18 aircraft — a smaller formation, a Flight, will be employed. It is perhaps convenient at this juncture to review briefly the RAF's organisation and nomenclature, in order that its obligations and methods may be better understood.

Subordinate to Parliament and the Joint Chiefs of Staff Committee, the RAF's chain of command begins with the Chief of Air Staff at the Ministry of Defence (Air) in Whitehall. Below this most senior officer are three major components: Strike Command, Support Command and RAF Germany. First of these to be encountered by the future pilot is Support Command, the responsibilities of which extend from selecting and training all officers and airmen, to supplying and maintaining their equipment and weaponry.

Most prominent of Support Command's assets (and deliberately so adorned to be conspicuous for safety reasons) is the 'Red and White Air Force' operated by Flying Training Schools and other specialist establishments. When much of the peacetime RAF closes for the weekend, Support Command's Bulldogs, Chipmunks and sailplanes will be found giving flying

Above:
It is only appropriate that No 617 Squadron, the 'Dambusters', should be equipped with the RAF's most advanced ever interdictor/strike aircraft, the Tornado GR1. The accuracy and destructive power of a single squadron of GR1s are as great as a wartime raid of over 500 Lancasters.

Below:
Phantom in the summer sun.

lessons to university students and taking aloft young men and women of the Air Training Corps and Combined Cadet Force — irrespective of whether or not they are committed to joining the Service.

Strike Command includes the 'teeth' of the RAF, in the form of a sizeable component of its front-line units. For administrative reasons these are sub-divided into three Groups responsible for different elements of operations. By far the largest, No 1 Group (with its HQ at Upavon, Wiltshire) is responsible for over-land strike/attack and reconnaissance, aerial refuelling and transport. Next in numerical sequence, No 11 Group is the historical descendant of Fighter Command and, indeed, still has its HQ at Bentley Priory, Stanmore, Middlesex, from where Air Chief Marshal Sir Hugh Dowding masterminded the Battle of Britain. All fighter-interceptor and SAM (surface-to-air missile) squadrons are administered by No 11 Group, as are the ageing Shackleton 'flying radar stations' which are used to spot low-level raiders.

Finally, No 18 Group is all which remains of the former Coastal Command. Its are the maritime reconnaissance aircraft and the high-profile yellow helicopters whose service to the civilian community is so much appreciated. Strike/attack aircraft speci-fically dedicated to naval duties (ie the Buccaneers, but not the Royal Navy's own Fleet Air Arm) are also within No 18. Administering Strike Command is the Air Officer Commanding-in-Chief, whose own head-quarters are at High Wycombe — the former home of the now defunct Bomber Command and its legendary wartime leader, Air Chief Marshal Sir Arthur Harris. The AOC-in-C also holds the NATO post of C-in-C United Kingdom Air Forces, which will be the title of the RAF if the Alliance command structure is fully activated in an emergency.

There is a also strong NATO connection in the last of the three main Commands: RAF Germany. Whereas Strike Command includes some advanced training formations (the Operational Conversion Units), RAFG is entirely devoted to combat roles. Almost exclus-ively equipped with Tornado GR1s (though also charged with providing medium helicopter support to the army), it is commanded by an RAF officer who also holds the NATO rank of C-in-C 2nd Allied Tactical Air Force. This is no mere ceremonial title, for 2 ATAF also includes the entire Belgian and Netherlands air forces, plus half of the Federal German Luftwaffe and a component of the US Air Force Europe. Thus, the northern half of NATO's air strength on the crucial Central Front is entrusted to British leadership.

The no-notice spot-checks on combat readiness (known as Tacevals) to which NATO submits all its units, confirm that the RAF component of 2 ATAF is ready to respond well within the required time. No less highly trained and prepared are the home-based units of Strike Command. For many squadrons, some aspects of wartime operation are an everyday occurrence as aircraft are operated out of the concrete hangarettes which shield them from a conventional bombing attack. More equipmnent and personnel are needed to sustain this detached existence, and both aircrew and servicing staff are regularly required to train wearing the uncomfort-able 'goon suits' and respirators which will provide protection against the massive Warsaw Pact supremacy in chemical and biological weapons.

Once airborne on a training flight, the combat pilot has much to do in addition to guiding his mount from A to B. Operating costs are such that the maximum instructional value must be wrung from every sortie, with the result that (say) a Tornado GR1 flight of about an hour's duration might include a simulated bombing run, evasion practice with interceptors and a refuelling rendezvous with a tanker. Pilots who claim that flying 'is their life' are exaggerating slightly: the NATO minimum for combat crew is just 180 hours airborne time per annum — and there are 8,760 hours in a year! However, the complexities of planning, de-briefing, simulator training, adminis-tration and myriad other responsibilities and duties ensure little leisure during the other hours of duty.

There remain advantages a-plenty to compensate for the pressures inherent in being entrusted with an immensely costly aircraft and, sometimes, weaponry of scarcely imaginable destructive power. Chief amongst these is the comradeship of fellow aviators — a bond so strong that diametrically opposed political ideologies cannot dissuade the interceptor pilot from exchanging a wave with the crew of a Soviet maritime reconnaissance aircraft as both go about their daily business. Having been one of the few both called and chosen to join that elite band, the author is privileged to present this unique, one-pilot's view of today's RAF.

PER ARDUA...

A Chipmunk T10 trainer on a Staff Continuation Training sortie flown by one of No 6 Air Experience Flight's Voluntary Reserve (VR) pilots over Lincolnshire. Although a 'low performance' aircraft, the Chipmunk presents quite a challenge when it comes to landing, which makes it an ideal aircraft for assessing the potential of new pilots.

Perched on the edge of the North Downs between London and the French coast, the village of Biggin Hill is largely indistinguishable from the dozens of other settlements scattered over the Kentish country-side. In one important respect, however, 'Biggin-on-the Bump' occupies an unchallenged position in history, for it is regarded by those Londoners with long-enough memories as 'their' RAF station. When the RAF was all which stood between Britain and invasion, it was the Hurricanes and Spitfires of Biggin and its neighbouring bases which fought at great odds against the Luftwaffe. The Battle of Britain was Hitler's first defeat — and it proved to be of greater consequence than all his previous victories.

Today, a handful of RAF bases continue to brave the uncertainties of autumnal weather and hold their open days on the Saturday nearest to 15 September in remembrance of the day in 1940 when the greatest claim of shot-down enemy aircraft was made. Biggin Hill is still playing a role in Britain's air defences, though the only aircraft which take off from its runways are light civilian machines flying for business or pleasure. In the remaining RAF enclave, young men aspiring to be aircrew are assessed for their suitability to join what is widely reckoned to be one of the most demanding training organisations in the world. Those who pass the rigorous tests for bodily co-ordination and leadership qualities leave Biggin Hill with a foothold on the long ladder which leads to a flying appointment in an operational squadron.

Biggin is a station of RAF Support Command, the component responsible for providing a broad range of back-up services to the two fighting arms, Strike Command and RAF Germany. Prospective pilots attend Support Command's training units to gain the skills of flying before being posted to a squadron, though in many cases an RAF career begins with at least three years at university, sponsored by the Service. During this time, up to 90 hours of flying is accumulated on the BAe Bulldog T1 with one of the 16 University Air Squadrons throughout the country before transfer to another historic RAF station: Cranwell, Lincolnshire. At the RAF College here, the young pilots encounter a jet trainer for the first time in the form of the BAe (previously BAC) Jet Provost, which they fly for some 80 hours in a 31-week course.

Alternatively, those not intending to make a lifetime career in the RAF may opt for direct entry, which omits the university stage. After their initial officer training, the first flying stage for candidates is at Swinderby, near Lincoln, where around 63 hours are flown on the ageing de Havilland Chipmunk T10s of the Elementary Flying Training Squadron. These students, too, progress next to Jet Provosts, with either No 1 Flying Training School at Linton-on-Ouse, or No 7 FTS at Church Fenton — both close to York — where 100 hours' flying is accumulated in 37 weeks.

Flying training is not intended to be easy, and each student must find his own way of relating to the challenge placed before him. It is as well that he acquires the mental discipline necessary to spur him on in the constant quest for perfection, as that will be expected from him on a daily basis on an operational squadron. Only in this way can the pilot hope to be able to meet the ultimate test of conflict should Britain's policy of deterrence ever fail.

The initial thrill of flying a propeller-driven Bulldog or Chipmunk can soon become forgotten in the round of daily lectures and flying. The exhilaration returns, however, when an acquaintance is made with the Jet Provost. First, there is the three-day aviation medicine course at North Luffenham to ensure that candidates are physically fit to fly high-performance aircraft. There are briefings and euphemistically-termed 'familiarisations' of such aspects as disorientation, vertigo, hypoxia (oxygen starvation), decompression and pressure breathing — to name but a few. Of all, perhaps the last-mentioned is the most un-nerving, as one relaxes to have oxygen forced into the lungs and must then exert force to breathe out.

Having endured all, the hopeful pilot leaves North Luffenham proudly clutching his personal issue 'bone dome' (flying helmet), feeling that he has at last 'arrived'. After another four weeks of ground school, learning Aerodynamics, Meteorology, Navigation, Maths and gaining a working knowledge of aircraft systems, it is time to step into a Jet Provost (universally known as the JP). The first sortie is a 'free' one for accustomisation; thereafter formal assessment by a Qualified Flying Instructor will be made every time the student takes to the air.

The cockpit seems an alien invironment for that first JP ride. The helmet feels tight and needs time to bed-in; the oxygen mask presses hard against one's cheeks and nose; strong straps pin the body firmly to the ejection seat; the comforting chugging of a piston engine is replaced by the whine of a jet. Seemingly oblivious to this unease, the instructor sits beside the student, calm and relaxed, conversing with air traffic control in a strange-sounding shorthand language which takes months to comprehend.

But confidence does gradually come to most of the students on the course. Following the basics of flight and the proud moment of a first 'solo' come the enjoyment of individual aerobatic manoeuvres and the combination of these into a routine to sharpen co-ordination of body and mind. Formation flying, too, is practised, but these skills are not acquired in order to provide a supply of pilots for the Red Arrows. All are vital steps in making the pilot feel at one with his aircraft, able to act instinctively and with confidence throughout the entire performance envelope of the machine. A further step towards this end comes with the start of instrument flying in cloud, when the pilot must learn to disregard the sometimes false signals transmitted by his senses and trust the dials and gauges on the instrument panel.

Stories are passed around of students being 'chopped' or 'washed-out' because they fail to achieve the exacting standards demanded, and each man privately assesses his own performance against that of his fellows, hoping not to find himself bottom of the class. It doesn't help to remember the adage that 50% of one's brain power is immediately lost when stepping into a cockpit during the early stages of basic jet training on the JP.

Even among those who display the exceptional qualities demanded of an RAF pilot, there are variations in aptitude. Accordingly, at the end of the basic flying stage, students are 'streamed' into one of three Groups for advanced instruction. Group 1, representing those suitable for fast-jet flying, stay at their FTS for up to 60 more hours of JP sorties before progressing to Valley, Anglesey, to fly the BAe Hawk. Group 2 — the future multi-engine fliers — have around 30 hours of extra JP tuition, then go to the Multi-Engine Training Squadron of No 6 FTS at Finningley, South Yorks, for 45 hours on BAe Jetstream T1s. Group 3 are the helicopter trainees, who are posted straight to No 2 FTS at Shawbury for a Gazelle and Wessex course.

In service since 1976, the Hawk T1 is a popular and capable advanced trainer, which has gained considerable overseas sales success — not least in the form of a US Navy commitment to buy over 300. In 23 weeks at Valley's No 4 FTS, students fly 75 hours in the aircraft (plus 21 more in a simulator), expanding their knowledge of advanced flying and touching on several primary aspects of combat operations. Faster than the JP, the Hawk forces the pupil to compress his thought processes, especially on the low-level missions which are an important aspect of military flying. It also differs in being a tandem-seat aircraft, not side-by-side like the Provost. In the view of some, the latter arrangement provides helpful moral support during early training, although in later stages it is better that the instructor can be less obtrusive in his position in the rear seat. The Shorts Tucano T1 turboprop, soon to replace the JP, will dispense with side-by-side seating entirely, and will also result in the student having to wait until the Hawk stage for his first jet flight.

By the end of the Valley course, pilots are flying almost by instinct, leaving some of their mental

Bottom:
The pilot of XW313 breaks away from close formation and is about to reposition for another join into close. During this exercise the student must come in with controlled overtake, sitting wide and slightly low on the lead aircraft. The skill is in judging the relative closure and in not overshooting.

Below:
Jet Provost T5A XW313 overflies Cranwel routine training sortie at medium level. W initio training course, its student pilot is subjected to a formation take-off, close fo manoeuvring, tail chasing and close form recovery — an hour's worth of sweaty ha Skills such as the formation manoeuvres units like those at Cranwell, Linton-on-O Church Fenton and are continually called throughout service flying.

capacity free for other things. It is now time for the Group 1 fliers to leave the 'Red and White Air Force' of Support Command and join the RAF's 'sharp end' where that surplus processing power will be quickly absorbed in learning to operate an aircraft and its systems as a fighting machine. On reporting to either No 1 or No 2 Tactical Weapons Units (at Brawdy, in southwest Wales, and across the Bristol Channel at Chivenor, Devon), the pilot finds the familiar Hawks awaiting him, except that these aircraft are camouflaged.

Brawdy has about 35 of the 175 Hawks delivered to the RAF, and Chivenor another 45. Fitted with a 30mm cannon beneath the fuselage and practice bombs under the wings, they are the vehicle for 54 hours of weapons training, during the second part of which there is again a streaming of students. Those who will later go into the offensive support world concentrate on surface attack techniques; others, assessed suitable for interceptor fighters, tend to receive more practice in air combat manoeuvring. Some of the Hawks have low-level green-and-grey camouflage, although many have received overall light grey medium-level markings. The latter colours are not just for realistic training, as 88 aircraft have been converted to Hawk T1A standard to carry two AIM-9L Sidewinder air-to-air missiles, and will form part of Britain's air defences in the event of war.

Not all who climbed into a JP for that first familiarisation sortie get out of a Hawk on termination of the TWU course. Some will be flying less demanding aircraft, or may even have re-roled as navigators or air electronics officers; others may now be addressed as plain 'Mister'. Yet still the training progresses relentlessly. Now knowing the type of aircraft he will fly on his first tour, the fully-qualified pilot begins training on that specific model at an Operational Conversion Unit, learning its flying characteristics and its capabilities in combat, working in close harmony with a navigator if it is a two-seater.

After over three years of high-pressure flying training and at a cost of £3.25 million, the RAF has gained a new pilot for a front-line squadron. Those who have been routed to multi-engine or helicopter flying have no reason to feel inferior, as each will have his abilities stretched to their safe limit during the years ahead. If the fighter pilot rocketing into the sky, bound to escort a Soviet reconnaissance bomber through UK airspace, had time for idle thought, he might reflect on the present activities of his course-mates from Cranwell, Linton or wherever. One might have a field gun slung beneath his helicopter whilst skimming over the West German countryside at night; another could be flying down a dead-end valley in Africa, piloting a Hercules transport laden with desperately-needed food. Each is the product of a training system which is the envy of the world.

13

Right:
Hawks at Valley. The yellow lines indicate the taxi directions to and from the active runway, while the thin rectangular boxes either side of the aircraft define the areas for ground support equipment, to minimise the risk of collision damage.

Far right:
Strapping-in in preparation for a formation sortie.

Below:
Hawk T1 XX296 has just started and is ready to taxi, with the instructor in the rear seat and student in the front. The canopy in the foreground shows the MDC (miniature detonating cord) which explodes and shatters the canopy during the ejection sequence.

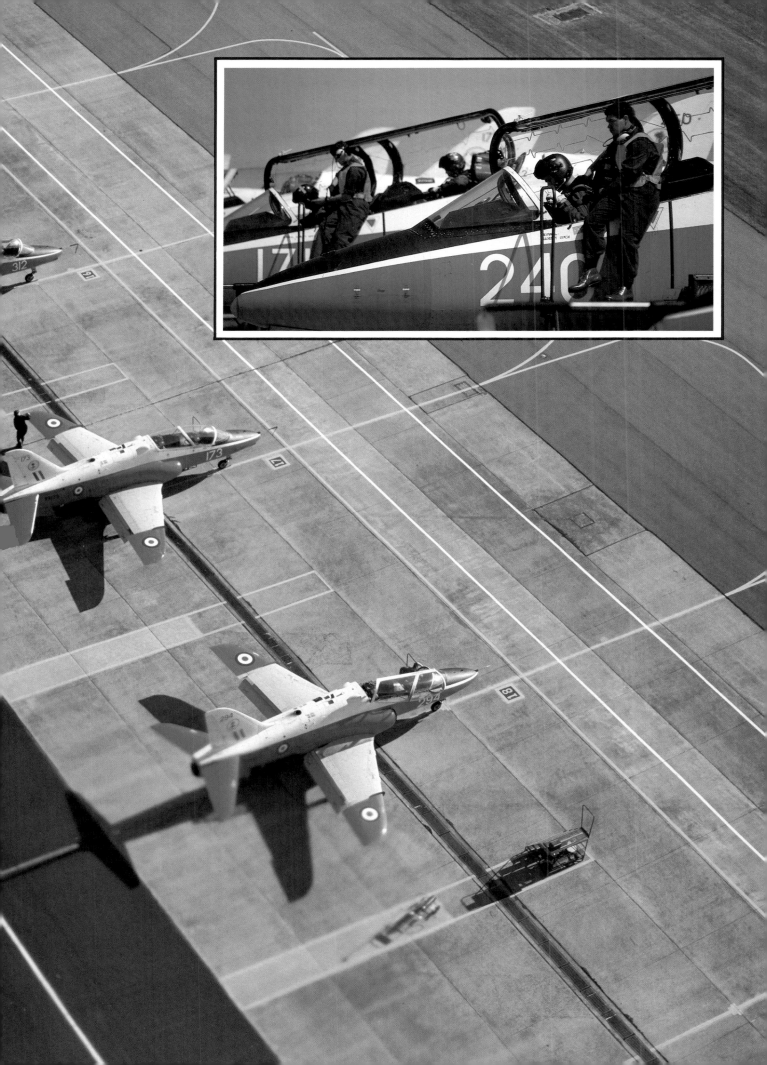

Left:
A dramatic view of a Hawk piloted by ex-Red Arrows 'Synchro' leader Sqn Ldr Phil Tolman.

Below:
The raspberry ripple paint scheme is used for training aircraft to aid detection at all levels, hopefully reducing the likelihood of collision.

Left:
Hawk T1 XX295, leader of a formation sortie, taxies out past No 2.

Right:
The formation moves to echelon port. The Hawk is easy to fly, yet can be demanding to fly accurately: its introduction has enabled the RAF to place the emphasis of training on later training needs and operational requirements.

Above:
No 1 TWU/No 234 Squadron Hawk T1A XX159 carries a 30mm Aden cannon pod as it flies at low level in the evening sun. The Tactical Weapons Unit aircraft provide weapons training for the fast-jet flyers. Note the vertical black lines below each canopy: these direct the pilot's feet to recesses for egress (for ground operations only!).

Below:
The Hawk features improved endurance and range compared to its predecessors, the Gnat and Hunter, and this has enabled more demanding sorties to be flown. Another benefit is illustrated by this No 1 TWU T1A, XX190. Fitted with Sidewinder air-to-air missiles, the aircraft can now play a significant role in air defence, too.

...AD ASTRA

Hurtling towards each other at a closing speed approaching that of sound, the two scarlet-painted aircraft appear to be heading for certain destruction. A fraction of a second before apparent disaster, both twist so their wings are vertical as they flash by with only feet to spare. Trailing a white ribbon of billowing smoke, the two Hawks rocket upwards into the clear blue sky, turning and descending more gently after reaching the limit of their climb. Necks craning, the crowd watches in wonder as seven more Hawks in perfect formation fly through the centre of the perfectly-shaped heart their fellows have drawn in the air.

Members of the public unable to tell a Tornado from a Tiger Moth instantly recognise the Red Arrows. Formed in 1965, the team has operated Hawks since 1980, and is currently based at Scampton, Lincs, as a component of the Central Flying School. CFS trains the RAF's flying instructors to perpetuate one of the world's most respected training courses, and the Red Arrows are the visible proof of the exceptional standard achieved. At around 120 venues each year — some of them abroad — the team provides its show-stopping performance, never failing to be what is known in theatrical circles as 'good box office'.

Each year, three of the nine pilots are returned to more normal flying duties and replaced by what are unofficially known as FNGs ('Flipping' New Guys). Competition is fierce for these coveted places and only after interviews and assessments of their previous flying career are the successful volunteers invited to join the world-famous team. Throughout the autumn and winter, the FNGs participate in a punishing schedule of training, involving up to three sorties per day, culminating in the team's display being inspected and approved for release by the C-in-C of Support Command.

Above:
The Spitfire Mk 19 in Normandy invasion stripes.

Above and right:
At some time or other most squadrons fly nine-ship formations, which isn't too demanding. However, none manage to retain the spectacular symmetry of the chosen formation during even mild manoeuvre. The 'Reds' spend a great deal of time and effort working to correctly 'fudge' formation position relative to the crowd. That's the impressive thing — they don't just fly formation but display the team.

Right:
A rare shot indeed — trailing the Red Arrows into RAF Scampton in May 1986, the author was lucky enough to be 'Red 11' with new team-member-to-be Flt Lt Spike Newbery. The team call this their battle break, running in as two vics of five — yes, 10 in total, don't forget Sqn Ldr Henry Ploszek, the Manager. 'We slotted in down the back and took a few cheap shots.'

Above:
The 1988 Red Arrows Team.

The Red Arrows may be said to demonstrate to the taxpayer that the RAF is providing the best possible service to its 'customers' in terms of training. Another team reminds air display spectators that it always has. Based at Coningsby, Lincs, the Battle of Britain Memorial Flight comprises a priceless collection of four Spitfires, two Hurricanes and a single Lancaster (plus a Chipmunk and a Devon — seemingly 'modern' equipment — for continuation training and communications). Flying hours are carefully conserved on these historic aircraft and their manoeuvring is stictly limited to avoid structural fatigue.

Nevertheless, at up to 150 displays per year, the nostalgic roar of six Rolls-Royce Merlins (or five and a Griffon) in unison is heard as the Lancaster, flanked by a Hurricane and Spitfire, echoes the RAF's former glories. The two fighters represent the aircraft which saved Britain and the Free World from tyrannical domination in 1940; the Lancaster recalls the 50,000 airmen in 9,000 bombers who failed to return from operations while ensuring the ultimate victory for democracy. Young spectators are thrilled to see such veterans being put through their paces, although some of an older generation just stand silently, sniffing back the tears.

Above:
'Synchro Leader' Flt Lt Ade Thurley in joking mood — 'who switched the lights out?'

Below:
Distinctive helmet and informal brief.

Below:
A Spitfire on the break at RAF Coningsby.

Left:

A Spitfire pair of the Battle of Britain Memorial Flight. Few people are lucky enough to get their hands on such rare aircraft as these — except for those on the BBMF or sporting a healthy bank balance.

Below:

The BBMF Lancaster from Coningsby in Lincolnshire. At present it is the only flying example in the world — but possibly not for long, as rumour has it that the ex-Strathallan Lanc may be restored to flying condition.

SUPER OMNIA UBIQUE

OVER ALL THINGS EVERYWHERE

No 82 Squadron

Above:
A No 84 Squadron Wessex carries out winching practice off the coast of Cyprus.

The night is pitch black; howling winds tear at the onlookers' clothes as they watch powerless from the clifftops. Again and again, the pitiless sea grasps the small trawler and dashes it against the rocks. Aboard, the fishermen grasp any hand-hold and hope against hope for rescue before their frail craft is smashed to matchwood. From the seaward, about at cliff height, a finger of brilliant light stabs out through the driving sleet: probing, feeling. Through the icy wind's roar — faintly at first, then with ever-increasing intensity — is heard the rhythmic, pulsating beat of helicopter rotors. Dimly visible, the yellow-painted craft fights to hover in the teeth of the gale as one of its crew, a Flight Sergeant, descends to the white foam below, suspended only by a perilously thin strand of wire. One by one the terrified and exhausted sailors are winched aboard and borne to safety beneath rotating wings, but for the helicopter crew the worst is yet to come. Surrounded by the press, squinting against the glare of TV lights, the Flight Sergeant has a microphone thrust under his nose. Red-faced and with a self-conscious shrug he replies to the barrage of questions, 'Just doing what we're trained for, I suppose'.

True though this modest answer may be, it conceals much. It is the SAR (Search & Rescue) task which captures the public's imagination when humanitarian duties are to be done — expectant mothers carried to hospital; snow-bound ponies fed on bleak Dartmoor — but the helicopter crew may find itself engaged in less well-publicised tasks, such as inserting SAS teams behind enemy lines in wartime.

For the pilot reporting to No 2 Flying Training School at Shawbury in Shropshire, such events seem far in the future. Helicopter flying instruction has small beginnings, and military helicopters don't come much smaller than the sprightly Anglo-French Gazelle HT3 which forms the first part of the No 2 FTS course. Designed by Aérospatiale and built at Yeovil and Weston-super-Mare by Westland, the Gazelle is a highly manoeuvrable machine with a very generous performance envelope. Capable of speeds up to 164mph (264km/hr) — quite a respectable pace for a helicopter — it serves all three armed services in the training role and additionally operates with the Army in the fields of liaison and observation.

Shawbury's fleet of 26 Gazelles provides the first 75-80 flying hours of instruction, during which the student fresh from Jet Provosts (or soon, the Tucano) learns the rudiments of rotary-wing operations. Once this Phase One is mastered, the switch is made to the other half of the No 2 FTS complement: Westland Wessex HC2s. Ten of these larger helicopters provide a follow-on course of 50 or so hours in a type representative of RAF operational equipment. It is during this phase that instructors begin to sense the

Right:
XR507, a Wessex HC2 of 'D' Flight, No 22 Squadron, based at Leconfield, moves in close to winch up a pilot on sea drill. Search and rescue (SAR) helicopters are no doubt a welcome sight when the alternative is a night at sea in a single-man dinghy. The Wessex displays the Squadron's unusual badge, a Maltese cross with a mathematical 'pi' sign overlaid.

Below:
Wessex HC2 XR528 'A' of No 28 Squadron RAF Sek Kong carries out policing duties over Hong Kong harbour.

Bottom:
XZ594, a 'B' Flight Sea King HAR3 of No 202 Squadron, stands on search and rescue alert at RAF Brawdy in southwest Wales.

student's aptitude for different branches of the helicopter world.

Wessex training in Phase Two has already given the pilot additional responsibility of flying with a crew, and at about half-way through the course he will be earmarked for SAR/Wessex or tactical (Puma/Chinook) duties on qualification. If it is to be the latter, the Gazelle is brought back for a 20-hour Phase Three course which is a most exhilarating addition to the 28-week programme at Shawbury. Acting as an introduction to the type of Army support work carried out daily in RAF Germany and elsewhere, Phase Three sees the newly-qualified pilot practising ultra-low level flying at a mere 5ft (1.5m) from the ground and using natural features such as trees and hills to conceal his approach to a landing area. When en route to a task, the normal procedure is to fly *under*, not over, high-tension cables.

Apart from four VIP transport HT3/HCC4s forming part of the equipment of No 32 Squadron at Northolt, West London, the Gazelle is restricted to training duties. Most 'non-combat' helicopter pilots will therefore begin their careers flying Wessex. This much-modified derivative of the Sikorsky S-58 is powered by a pair of turboshaft engines and was once the standard Army support helicopter, until eclipsed by later designs. Deliveries of 72 Wessex HC2s were effected between 1963 and 1968, and just over 60 remain in service.

About 20 are assigned to No 22 Squadron for SAR — easily identifiable because of their brilliant yellow colour schemes. Rescue techniques are a specialised area, so pilot and crewmen attend a course at the SAR Training Unit at Valley, Anglesey, to learn the many and varied skills required. As well as being on the coast, Valley is conveniently close to Snowdonia, as an SAR call-out (of which there are about 1,000 per year) might just as easily involve rescuing an injured mountaineer as lifting a seaman from an endangered vessel. Strictly speaking, the SAR helicopter force is there to rescue downed airmen, the hundreds of civilians it saves from near-certain death every year being merely 'practice'.

The centre of RAF SAR operations is Finningley, in South Yorkshire. It is here that No 22 Squadron has its HQ and overhaul facilities, although five operational flights are positioned around the coast at Chivenor (Devon), Leuchars (Fife), Valley, Leconfield (Humberside) and Manston (Kent) — respectively 'A' to 'E' Flights. Filling in the gaps, as it were, is No 202 Squadron, also headquartered at Finningley. Since 1978, No 202 has been flying the Westland Sea King HAR3, a larger helicopter of far greater potential than the Wessex.

Also based on a Sikorsky design, it possesses greater range and has improved electronic aids for all-weather operation. The Sea King can reach farther out to sea than its smaller brother and has the invaluable addition of radar for navigation and location. Most of the 19 delivered are based at Boulmer (Northumberland), Brawdy (Dyfed), Coltishall (Norfolk) and Lossiemouth (Moray) with 'A' top HU 'D' Flights respectively. In sunnier climes, Wessex undertake SAR and Medevac (medical evacuation) tasks with No 84 Squadron at the sovereign base of Akrotiri in Cyprus — though these are HU Mk 5Cs borrowed from the Navy — and with No 28 Squadron in Hong Kong. The remaining squadron is No 72 at Aldergrove, Northern Ireland. No 84 is additionally responsible for assisting the United Nations peacekeeping forces in Cyprus and No 72 has the not dissimilar task of supporting the Army in the troubled Province. Perhaps the only Wessex flying which the newly-qualified pilot will most certainly not be invited to undertake is that reserved for the highly experienced crews of The Queen's Flight at Benson, south of Oxford, where two VIP Wessex HCC4s are on charge.

Below:
The cockpit readiness state of an SAR Sea King. In front of the seats are the cycle sticks, and to the left of the seats are the collective pitch levers. On the interseat console are the flying and navigation aids such as TANS (Tactical Air Navigation System), while the instrument panel displays status instruments — airspeed, altitude, fuel, engine temperature, pressure, etc.

A cloak of matt green-and-grey camouflage adorns the helicopters whose business is war. Unarmed, save for an optional light machine-gun in the cabin doorway, the Puma and Chinook are assigned to operate closely with the Army wherever it may be deployed. Another Anglo-French product, the Aérospatiale-Westland Puma HC1 entered service in 1971, deliveries totalling 48 British-built helicopters to the RAF. The normal load is up to 16 troops or 2½ tons of cargo, the latter stowed internally or as an underslung load. Such a useful capability pales into insignificance against the twin-rotor American Boeing-Vertol Chinook HC1, which will carry 44 seated troops or 12 tons of cargo. As is often recounted, the single Chinook which operated with distinction during the Falklands War lifted over 80 soldiers (standing room only!) on one remarkable flight.

RAF Odiham proclaims itself to be 'The Home of the Battlefield Helicopter' and it is from this Hampshire station that No 33 Squadron flies 18 Pumas and No 7 a dozen Chinooks. (Also resident is No 240 Operational Conversion Unit with five of each for training.) These British-based helicopters are assigned to support rapid deployment forces of the Army: units which may be dispatched at short notice to bolster NATO's flanks in Norway or the strategically important entrance to the Baltic through Danish territory. Accordingly they are outfitted to operate from dispersed sites in the field — living under canvas and servicing their machines in the open.

Five Chinooks and three grey-painted SAR Sea Kings are based with No 78 Squadron on the Falkland Islands and four more Pumas form No 1563 Flight in the Central American protectorate of Belize, but the remainder of the battlefield helicopter force is assigned to RAF Germany for the use of No 1 (BR) Corps, BAOR. Stationed at Gütersloh, which is the

only RAF airfield east of the Rhine, are No 18 Squadron with 12 Chinooks and No 230 Squadron operating 16 Pumas. In all the RAF has received 41 Chinooks since 1980.

When called to action, the helicopters foresake their base for the North German Plain, small groups of four or five taking up positions perhaps in the corner of a field, close to woods or farm buildings. Pumas are based closest to the battle line, the Chinooks just behind — but still farther forward than the Harriers. Each detachment has its Flight Control Centre (mounted on the back of a truck) which is in contact by radio and dispatch rider with the Air Support Operations Centre (ASOC) located alongside HQ No 1 Corps. ASOC delegates tasks to the Chinooks and Pumas according to availability and capability: perhaps some fuel and ammunition to be delivered here; a complete Rapier surface-to-air missile fire unit and its crew (in and beneath a Chinook) moved there. As the outnumbered NATO forces cannot be everywhere at once, helicopters might be used to deploy quick reaction teams to neutralise Warsaw Pact sabotage parties (Spetsnaz) infiltrated behind Allied lines.

At times when hostile aircraft are prowling, and infantrymen with potent, shoulder-launched anti-aircraft missiles are possibly lurking, the tactical flying of Phase Three at Shawbury comes to the fore. In their journeys to the battle lines to carry in supplies and extract wounded, the helicopters will use every scrap of cover to mask their movements, being especially careful to avoid overflying lakes and

Above:
Whereas fixed-wing pilots go from the Jet Provost to the Hawk, helicopter pilots move on to the Gazelle at the start of helicopter training. Here Gazelle HT3 ZA803 'X' of No 2 FTS at Shawbury is seen accompanied by a Dakota of the Royal Aircraft Establishment at Farnborough.

Top:
A No 230 Squadron Puma on underslung-load-carrying training at Gutersloh in West Germany. No 230, which first flew the Puma in 1971, is employed mainly in support of British Army operations in Germany.

reservoirs which will immediately negate their camouflage. Since the Falklands War, helicopter pilots have been receiving training in fighter evasion, assisted by the fitment of radar warning receivers which alert the crew to the fact that a hostile radar is monitoring the aircraft. Perhaps the best form of protection is to 'put down' until the danger has passed, rather than engage in one-sided combat. When on the ground between missions, helicopters are too large to be pushed across fields into cover, yet sacking over the cockpit transparencies will prevent the tell-tale glinting which would attract a fighter-pilot's eye.

Modern wars do not stop at sunset. Equipped with night-flying goggles, the pilot will continue his tasking in complete darkness. Even if chemical agents are employed by the enemy, the crew will don respirators in order to keep flying. Brief respite from this uncomfortable protective equipment can be gained within the confines of a plastic tent called a 'Porton Liner' which is inflated with filtered air and entered via an air-lock. Even without the inconvenience of 'country living' it is no exaggeration to say that operating a large helicopter like the Chinook into a battle zone is a task only slightly less demanding than flying a fast jet. Though he may not appreciate the finer points of aviation, the infantryman on the ground is no less grateful for the timely arrival of supplies and reinforcements from the air. To soldiers short of ammunition and food, no sound is more welcome than the throbbing beat of the twin-rotor known to every squaddie as 'The Big Wokka-Wokka'.

Above:
No 18 Squadron Chinook HC1 ZA670 'BS' operating to the south of Kemble in July 1982.

Below:
Chinook ZA670 loads up at RAF Gutersloh in 1985. A No 4 Squadron Harrier GR3 shelter stands in the background.

ANYWHERE

USQUAM

No 70 Squadron

Below and right:
A Lightning escorts No 47 Squadron Hercules C3P XV304 into Cyprus. The 'stretched' Herc was delivering spares for No 11 Squadron's Armament Practice Camp in September 1986.

With crew and aircraft ranged proudly on deck, the two aircraft carriers and their escorts nosed out of harbour and into the Solent. It was 5 April 1982 — just three days after an Argentine force had landed virtually unopposed on the Falkland Islands — and it seemed that the entire population of Portsmouth had turned out to pay tribute to what it believed was the vanguard of the Island's recovery force. When the weather is clear, it is possible from Portsmouth to see air traffic departing the airways reporting point at Ibsley on the opposite side of the Solent. During those previous three days, any of the historic naval town's citizens with an airband radio and the appropriate knowledge would have been aware of a steady procession of transports announcing their southerly departure from Ibsley, using call-signs prefixed 'ASCOT'. Within hours of the invaders' dramatic arrival, four Hercules of the Lyneham Transport Wing (Nos 24, 30, 47 and 70 Squadrons, and No 242 OCU) had lifted off from their Wiltshire base, bound for Gibraltar and Ascension Island.

These were the true leaders of the Task Force, though — as usual — little was heard of their exploits. Next day, the majestic jet-powered VC10 C1s of No 10 Squadron from Brize Norton in Oxfordshire began supporting Operation 'Corporate', and a steadily increasing number of Lyneham's fleet was drawn in to sustain the air bridge to Ascension. Each was carrying equipment needed by the Task Force or by those responsible for supporting it. But for the fact that this time it was 'for real', there was little unusual in the movement of the transports. All modern military operations — not least training deployments — require a vast back-up organisation and an uninterrupted line of communications back to base. Transport aircraft carry advanced stores to the

Left:
Hercules flightdeck. The crew XV299 of the Lyneham Transport Wing are (left) Captain Flt Lt Grant and (centre) co-pilot Flg Off Stilwell.

Below:
The Hercules' flightdeck in red-out prior to special operations at low level and at night.

Right and inset:
The VC10s of No 10 Squadron Brize Norton give the RAF a flexible passenger and freight capability. Here C1 XR810 is seen unloading at RAF Decimomannu in Sardinia.

Below right:
A VC10 navigator checks over the flight log prior to updating the Captain en route from RAF Akrotiri in Cyprus to Brize Norton.

intended destination; airlift in the force; and sustain it during its time abroad — or, as one transport pilot summed it up, 'Without us, nobody goes anywhere!'

Hercules and VC10s are merely part of the RAF's 'slow-jet' force, which also includes the maritime reconnaissance Nimrod and the Victor and TriStar tankers, as well as smaller aircraft like Dominies and Canberras. Once converted at the Multi-Engine Training School, Finningley, a pilot may find himself flying any of these aircraft, according to individual suitability and available vacancies. A course at the appropriate type Conversion Unit will result in qualification as second pilot for the larger aircraft types, quite possibly the Lockheed Hercules. Most of the RAF's 66 Hercules C1s received in the mid-1960s remain in daily service, 30 of them recently

'stretched' to C Mk 3 standard with the insertion of an extra 15ft (4.57m) of hold length. Several have gained a 'P' suffix to their designation, indicating addition of an aerial refuelling receiver probe for extra-long flights to the Falklands.

Regular services are flown to British bases overseas, though the majority of sorties are specially arranged, sometimes at short notice. The army is a major customer for RAF transport services, taking 70% of capacity and demanding more than an airline type of operation. Capable of lifting 19 tons or 92 troops (128 in C3 form), the Hercules may be used for the spectacular LAPES (Low-Altitude Parachute Extraction System) method of delivering large items such as Land Rovers and freight without stopping, or even touching the ground. With rear loading ramp

Below:
This E Mk 3 Andover of No 115 Squadron is employed on calibration duties and is seen at RAF Binbrook. The E Mk 3 is used primarily for flight checking the service's ground-to-air navigation facilities.

down, the Hercules approaches the dropping zone at around 10ft (3m) and releases a parachute attached to the load. The latter is then snatched out of the hold as the transport leaps into the air, relieved of its burden. Less well known are the exploits of the Hercules detailed to support the SAS in such techniques as free-fall parachuting of small teams behind enemy lines.

Complementing No 10 Squadron's 13 VC10 transports at Brize Norton are two other marks of the same aircraft, flown by No 101 Squadron since its reformation in 1984. The VC10 K2 and K3 are tanker aircraft assigned to AAR (Air-to-Air Refuelling) in partial replacement of the dwindling fleet of converted Victor K2s — formerly part of the V-Bomber force — at Marham, Norfolk. Nine tanker VC10s, which are identifiable by their hemp-coloured paintwork, have been augmented from early 1986 by the first of a similar number of Lockheed TriStars, issued to No 214 Squadron at Brize Norton. Adaptations of wide-bodied civil airliners, the TriStars were purchased as a result of the need to maintain a Falklands garrison — or more accurately, to retain a minimum resident force which can be quickly strengthened in an emergency. TriStars are both tankers and passenger transports, two of them being earmarked for further adaptation to freighters, with large doors to admit bulky loads. If the Islands are again threatened, TriStars will be able to bring troops and supplies within hours, whilst simultaneously refuelling a pair of fighters on the journey south.

Though half-a-dozen Hercules can function as tankers (mainly in the Falklands area with No 1312 Flight), it is with the VC10 and Victor that the majority of fast jet pilots will be familiar. Interceptors escorting a Soviet reconnaissance aircraft, or fighter-bombers off to Canada for low-level training — all will at some time have need of an AAR aircraft. When training for war, 'hook-ups' with the tanker are made without radio contact, calling for accurate navigation from all concerned. Orbiting in a 'race-track' pattern at the appointed rendezvous, the tanker is approached by the fighters from behind and begins trailing its hose. Signalling with what looks like a set of miniature traffic lights, it directs each aircraft either to the outer wing hoses or one deployed from the belly. Carefully, the fighters manoeuvre their AAR probes into the 'basket' at the end of the hose — a difficult task in turbulent air — and fuel flow begins automatically once the connection has been correctly made. Topped-up, they disengage and take up position on the tanker's starboard wingtip until cleared to resume their mission.

Economies have reduced the number of smaller transport aircraft available for communications, leaving HS Andovers and 125s as the main VIP aircraft. The Queen's Flight at Benson, Oxon, has a pair of BAe146s as the pride of its fleet, supported in fixed-wing flying by a single Andover CC2. The other five CC2s serve either No 32 Squadron at Northolt, Middlesex, or the RAF Germany communications squadron, No 60, at Wildenrath, augmented by three rear-loading Andover C1 former cargo transports. No 242 OCU at Brize is responsible for most transport crew conversion.

Apart from helicopters, No 32 Squadron operates a dozen BAe125 executive jets on military and government business. Outwardly similar, but in red training colours instead of white and grey transport markings, are the 20 Dominie T1s flown on navigator training exercises by No 6 FTS at Finningley. Requirements for realistic instruction see the Dominies making flights abroad to such places as Berlin and Gibraltar. Even more well travelled are the seven Andover E3s of Benson-based No 115 Squadron which are equipped to check the RAF's electronic navigation and landing aids throughout the globe.

Delivered from 1966 onwards, the Andovers are still young compared with that doyen of slow jets, the BAC Canberra. As the RAF's first jet bomber, the

Canberra entered service in 1951, though it is now used only in supporting roles. Surviving aircraft are concentrated at Wyton, near Huntingdon, in three units, of which No 100 Squadron has 20 of various marks to provide target facilities for all three armed services. Acting the part of enemy aircraft, or towing fabric targets for gunnery, No 100's aircraft are complemented by a dozen Canberra T17/17As of No 360 Squadron. The T17, with its extended nose seemingly covered in warts, trains air defence operators by jamming their radars and communications in the way in which an enemy would most surely do in an attempt to sow confusion. Finally, there are the six high-altitude Canberra PR9s of No 1 Photo-Reconnaissance Unit, used for survey work.

At Britain's extremities — St Mawgan, near Newquay, and Kinloss, Moray — is to be found another slow jet of illustrious ancestry. With a good memory and a little imagination it is easy to recognise the BAe Nimrod MR2 as a much-modified descendant of the world's first jet transport, the de Havilland Comet. Fitted with a weapons bay below the original pressurised fuselage and crammed with sophisticated sensing and processing equipment, the Nimrod daily scours Britain's waters and patrols far out into the Atlantic. Well known for its humanitarian activities, the aircraft appropriately named after the 'Mighty Hunter' of the Book of Genesis is optimised for probing the depths in search of submarines and destroying them with depth charges and torpedoes.

Even in peacetime, the locations of the massive Soviet submarine force are of great interest to NATO, for changes in the deployment pattern might herald the onset of increased tension between East and West. If war threatens, the Atlantic will become an immense conveyor belt for supplies from the US,

Far left:
Close aboard and plugged in to a VC10 refuelling tanker of No 101 Squadron, Brize Norton, is Lightning F6 XR773 of No 5 Squadron, RAF Binbrook. Lightning No 2 awaits its turn on the port side.

Top left:
Having been cleared behind to plug in, a Lightning closes on the port basket of a No 101 Squadron VC10.

Centre left:
A beautiful shot of a Jaguar in contact on the port side of a Victor K2. The day-glo lines under the Victor's wings are used as reference marks for inexperienced receivers.

Bottom left:
Buddy-buddy tanker operations. Topping up one tanker allows it to continue for a longer patrol time.

Left:
This illustration displays clearly the distinctive bulge of the Victor's forward fuselage, and the smooth manner in which the refuelling probe extends from the fuselage lines.

Below:
No 206 Sqn Nimrod MR2P XV239 is here being flown by crew 6 of RAF Kinloss, captained by Flt Lt Hugh Stewart. The following month crew 6 were scheduled to make the first in-service firings of the Harpoon air-to-sea missile.

Left:
Close up of the cockpit area of a Nimrod MR2P with power connected, refuelling probe uppermost and a viewing porthole on the port side. Portholes like these are removable and assist the Nimrod's day and night photo-recce role.

Below:
Thought by psychologists to be the most striking colour contrast, yellow and black spells danger within the service. Here No 100 Squadron's Canberra TT18 WJ680 uses the scheme to stand out from the ground in its role of target-towing for ground fire. Canberras fulfil a variety of roles, and this aircraft was in fact photographed on 'silent' target duties with fighter aircraft.

Far right:
The distinctive dorsal radome of Boeing's E-3 Sentry will soon be a regular feature of operations from RAF Waddington. Once AWACS is integrated into the air defence effort, the ageing Shackletons will at last be retired.

requiring Nimrods and their companions from allied countries to throw a protective screen around vital convoys. Each day, the Nimrod fleet of Nos 120, 201 and 206 Squadrons from Kinloss and No 42 Squadron and No 236 OCU at St Mawgan plays airborne cat to the Russians' underwater mouse, rehearsing for roles neither side wishes to act in earnest.

Highly efficient in their patrolling of the ocean's vast tracts, the RAF's 34 Nimrod MR2s should not be confused with the AEW3 version of the same four-jet, cancelled in 1986 as the result of protracted development problems with its vastly different suite of electronics. AEW — Airborne Early Warning — seeks to extend the range of defensive radars by carrying them high into the heavens instead of merely perching them on hilltops for a better view. Spotting incoming raiders seeking concealment by flying low over the earth's surface requires complex processing of radar signals to eliminate false returns, but the result is a range of 230 miles (370km) instead of only to the ground observer's horizon, and more time to organise a 'welcoming committee'.

NATO has been operating a force of 18 Boeing E-3A Sentry AWACS (Airborne Warning & Control System) aircraft since 1982, and with the demise of the Nimrod AEW3, the RAF is to acquire at least six of the same type from 1991 onwards. Until then, Britain's last front-line propeller-driven aircraft — six ageing Shackletons of No 8 Squadron at Kinloss — will continue to provide a limited service with their wholly obsolete AEW radar. When the Sentry AEW1 is firmly installed at its intended operating base of Waddington, Lincoln, its powerful and all-seeing eye will add a new dimension to the United Kingdom's security and open a fresh chapter in RAF history.

TUTOR ET ULTOR

PROTECTOR AND AVENGER

No 73 Squadron

Above:
A 'Battle' Flight Phantom FGR2 at Wildenwrath, West Germany, fully armed with four Sky Flash radar-guided missiles, four infra-red Sidewinders and a SUU-23/A pod containing a GAU-4 Vulcan 20mm cannon. As pilot Flt Lt Steve Ward and navigator Flt Lt Mike Pugh clamber in, XV460 is at bare minutes readiness.

The doors of the small hangar near to the runway's end open to reveal pilots and navigators climbing into their two fighters as ground crew hasten to strap them in and extract locking pins from the ejection seats. Out also come the safety locks from the flying controls, each marked with a red flag so it cannot be overlooked. The yellow 'Noddy caps' protecting the delicate seeker heads of four Sidewinder air-to-air missiles on each aircraft are removed. A further four missiles — this time long-range, all-weather Sky Flashes — nestle beneath the fuselage. Engines whine into life and the umbilical cord of the ground power unit is pulled from its socket in the fuselage. Out of the hangar roll two of Britain's air defence fighters, lurching in turn as pilots make a quick check on the brakes.

With priority over all other movements, the pair turn on to the runway and select full power without a pause. After a few seconds the engine note appears to hiccup, then adds an even more deafening, rasping overtone as the afterburner cuts in. Wheels are tucked away within moments of lift-off as, still trailing flame, the duo turns sharply north. Clearing the circuit they change radio frequency.

Miles away, deep underground, a voice answers: 'Yes, we have you on radar. Trade is approximately 62° north, 1° east, heading 230, flight level 250. Turn left 340 for intercept.' In the brilliant light above cloud, the target is visible for miles as the fighters close-in, formating on its wingtip. It is a 'Bear' — a Tupolev Tu-142 turboprop-powered, long-range maritime surveillance aircraft of the Soviet Navy — passing between the Shetlands and Faroes on a regular and perfectly legal reconnaissance mission. Crews exchange friendly waves as unannounced visitor and unrequested escort settle down to accompanying each other until the Russians leave UK airspace. Soon, someone else is joining the party. A VC10 tanker heaves into view, ready to replenish the thirsty fighters for as long as is necessary.

Unremarked by the media, the scene is repeated over 200 times per year as RAF fighters investigate Soviet aircraft transiting the UK Air Defence Region. Four million square miles of airspace extending almost to Iceland is Britain's responsibility, and all incoming aircraft which have not filed a flight plan must be investigated. Of course, in a time of normal political relations, it is unlikely that one Soviet bomber in international airspace presents a threat — but allowing them to 'get away with it' encourages adventurism. The more it becomes known throughout the Soviet Air Force that the RAF always finds its target — day or night, fine or cloudy — the stronger is the West's deterrent.

Strike Command's No 11 Group is in the process of completing a far-ranging modernisation of the entire air defence network, literally from under the ground upwards. Complementing new radars and refurbished control centres is the Panavia Tornado F3, a twin-engined, long-range, all-weather fighter intended to catch raiders far out to sea, before they can launch their cruise missiles against British targets. Deliveries of 162 air defence Tornados began late in 1984, the first 18 being to a slightly lower standard, designated F2.

Tornado — product of collaboration with West Germany and Italy — is equipped with an internal 27mm Mauser cannon for close engagements, though it is optimised for shooting down the enemy when he is still far out of visual range. Two types of missile are employed for this task, the smaller being the 10-mile (16km) range AIM-9L Sidewinder which homes on to heat generated by the target. Stretching out its reach to beyond 31 miles (50km) is Sky Flash, a weapon which follows signals bounced off the target by the fighter's radar.

First with Tornado fighters was No 229 OCU at Coningsby, Lincs, which was declared operational early in 1987 with the 'shadow' identity of No 65 Squadron. A 'shadow' is the title the unit would take if called into action, its aircraft flown by instructors in the manner of any full-time front-line squadron. Coningsby will house two more Tornado F3 units, Nos 29 (ex-Phantoms) and 5 (ex-Lightnings), before deliveries begin to Leeming, North Yorks, and Leuchars, Fife. Three squadrons (including No 11) will eventually reside at Leeming, whilst the Scottish base plans to replace the Phantoms of Nos 43 and 111 Squadrons.

Older in the tooth, but still respected, the McDonnell-Douglas Phantom carries a similar missile armament to the Tornado, but has to fit a cannon pod under the fuselage when such a weapon is required. Around 135 Phantoms remain from late-1960s deliveries (including 37 at Leuchars built to Royal Navy specifications as FG Mk 1s), plus 14 surplus US Navy F-4J(UK) models supplied in 1984 to No 74 'Tiger' Squadron at Wattisham, Suffolk. The latter replaced the Phantom FGR2s of No 23 Squadron based on the Falklands, the other overseas FGR2 units being Nos 19 and 92, which defend German airspace from Wildenrath. Finally there are No 56 Squadron with Mk 2s at Wattisham, which will accompany No 74 as the sole home operators of the aircraft until airframe lives are exhausted, and No 228 OCU ('shadow' No 64 Squadron) at Leuchars.

Time is rapidly running out, however, for the venerable BAC Lightning F6 which, in an earlier form, became Britain's first doubly-supersonic interceptor in 1960. With only two heat-seeking missiles, two cannon and a radar unable to detect targets below it, the Lightning now represents obsolescent technology. Almost 40 of the type are based at Binbrook alongside a handful of T5 two-seaters, shared by Nos 5 and 11 Squadrons. The former stood down for Tornado conversion in November 1987 and No 11

Above:
Intercept. Nos 43 and 111 Squadron FG1s move to investigate an unidentified intruder into the UK Air Defence Region.

Right:
FG1s of No 111 Squadron cruise north after a joint intercept mission with the author, against several mud-moving ingressors.

Far right:
A three-ship vic of the Lightning Training Flight and Nos 5 and 11 Squadrons powers out over the Humber estuary. This three-ship formation will never be seen again, because No 11 is re-forming with Tornado F3s.

ceased to be declared to SACEUR in April 1988. This will mean that for the first time, Britain will not have a wholly indigenous fighter in the front line ...

... unless one counts the BAe Hawk T1A. In 1986, BAe completed conversion of 88 of these agile advanced trainers to carry a pair of AIM-9L Sidewinders, enabling a force of 72 to be available for emergency use in point-defence or as part of the Mixed Fighter Force (MFF). Normally assigned to weapons training at Brawdy and Chivenor, Hawks already wear the markings of their 'shadow' squadrons: Nos 79 and 234 for No 1 TWU; Nos 63 and 151 for No 2 TWU.

Lacking radar and only just supersonic in a dive, the Hawk has the compensating advantage over most other warplanes in terms of manoeuvrability. In the MFF concept, Phantoms or Tornados will shepherd Hawks (also retaining the belly-mounted 30mm cannon pods) in offshore patrols, directing their small, tight-turning companions to break up incoming formations. Enemy aircraft which attempt to use superior speed to escape will fall victim to the large fighters and their long-range missiles. Making use of a tanker orbiting nearby, Phantoms and Tornados which have not 'fired out' (used-up their missiles and shells) will be able to stay on station for any follow-up attack.

A pilot will be only too aware that enemy surface-to-air missiles (SAMs) can result in his survival drills becoming a vital necessity, yet he can take some consolation in the fact that the RAF has its own similar defences. Such missiles will never replace fighter aircraft (the 1957 Defence White Paper prophesied they would — but we are still waiting), yet they have a useful role to play in augmenting the air defences of No 11 Group. Between the Thames and the Humber, Nos 25 and 85 Squadrons operate a chain of six sites equipped with BAC Bloodhound 2 SAMs, providing the means to destroy aircraft at all operating heights. The subject of ongoing modernisation, Bloodhound will remain in use well into the 1990s.

Point defence is the responsibility of the RAF Regiment. Formed in 1942 with a specific responsibility for airfield protection, the Regiment retains an identical brief today, providing troops to guard perimeter fences and Harrier field bases as well as anti-aircraft guns and SAMs. In fact the only guns in use today are the radar-directed Oerlikon 35mm weapons seized on the Falklands and operated by No 2729 Squadron at Waddington.

The BAe Rapier SAM has been the standard method of stopping low-level aircraft attacking certain RAF bases since 1974, although by no means all stations

are thus defended. The Scottish airfields of Leuchars and Lossiemouth are assigned Nos 27 and 48 Squadrons, whilst all four main bases in Germany have Rapier: No 16 Squadron at Wildenrath; No 26 at Laarbruch; No 37 at Brüggen; and No 63 at Gütersloh. Every unit now has the Blindfire model of Rapier which is capable of engaging aircraft at night or in bad weather after first confirming their identity by interrogating the IFF (Identification Friend or Foe) radio transmitter carried by all Allied aircraft. Squadrons comprise eight mobile launchers, each with eight men, plus HQ and engineering support components.

Throughout the day, and every day of the year, Phantoms, Lightnings and Tornados stand guard, ready for the order to intercept an unannounced aircraft appearing on radar screens. This (as described above) is the Quick Reaction Alert (Intercept) force — QRA(I), or just 'Q' for short. There are Northern and Southern divisions to the task; the former, which gets the lion's share of trade, is always the responsibility of two aircraft drawn from the Leuchars squadrons. Southern QRA is taken in turns by Binbrook, Coningsby and Wattisham.

Should No 11 Group again be called to defend Britain against air attack, the battle it fights will have

Left:
This was an extremely rare sight: not the paint scheme — although it was non-standard — but more so the F3 Lightning. This particular bird sports the markings of the now disbanded Lightning Training Flight (LTF). Following the graduation of the last student (Flt Lt Ian Black) in February 1987 and the disbandment of the LTF in April 1987, the end of the Lightning's days with the RAF became imminent and all the Lightning F3s are now withdrawn from service.

Below:
' "Fox 2" kill, closing for guns' — a Lightning F3 launches a Firestreak.

Left:
Not just an ordinary echelon to port formation on this Lightning F6, but flown in a two-seat Lightning from the right-hand seat. Unlike the ordinary left-hand throttle/right-hand control, the two-seat Lightning has the controls reversed in the right-hand seat. This makes initial training in the right-hand seat somewhat different for instructors: imagine the potential confusion at night, formating on a tanker in turbulence.

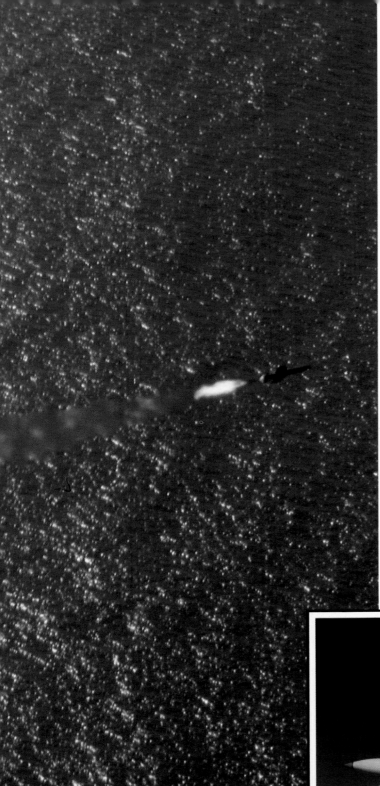

only superficial similarities to the historic conflict of 1940. Enemy aircraft will not obligingly form up in gigantic circuses at medium altitude over France before beginning their assault, as did the Luftwaffe. Warsaw Pact strike aircraft and bombers will fly low over the sea, below the horizon of ground-based radars. The longer-ranged of them will operate from Arctic bases and fly circuitous routes over the Atlantic to attack from the rear, where they hope to find lower standards of defence. Maximum use will be made of stand-off weapons in an attempt to evade fighters altogether, and those which are intercepted will vigorously employ electronic countermeasures to put out the defenders' radar 'eyes'.

But NATO has not been idle in the face of these developments. Like their strike/attack companions, interceptors are lodged in reinforced concrete hangarettes, known as Hardened Aircraft Shelters (HAS), for security against conventional attack. And if he tries to sneak in via the 'back door', the enemy will find Tornados deployed to Stornoway, in the Hebrides. Most importantly of all, however, have been the improvements in electronics since the days of the Lightning.

The Phantom features pulse-Doppler radar with the vital characteristic that it can look down in order to spot intruders against the 'clutter' generated by surface echoes. Sky Flash missiles can be fired against the target, even if he is flying as low as a few hundred feet. In the Tornado F3, this look-down/shoot-down capability is augmented by track-while-scan (TWS) and fitment of a JTIDS terminal. TWS means, simply, that the radar can keep careful track of a potential target whilst continuing to search for others. The intended victim's radar warning receiver

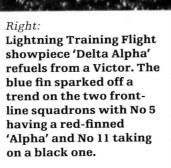

Right:
Lightning Training Flight showpiece 'Delta Alpha' refuels from a Victor. The blue fin sparked off a trend on the two front-line squadrons with No 5 having a red-finned 'Alpha' and No 11 taking on a black one.

Right:
Equipped with the AIM-9L Sidewinder, the Hawk T1A now plays a significant role in the UK's air defence. Tactical use of the Hawk's Sidewinder AAM is exercised annually at the Air Combat Manoeuvring Installation (ACMI) in Decimomannu, Sardinia. This No 234 Squadron Hawk, flown by Flt Lt Pete Jon, is returning to Deci following a two-versus-two against USAF F-15 Eagles.

Below:
Not all Tactical Weapons Unit Hawks are light grey. This No 234 Squadron aircraft carries the AIM-9L Sidewinder acquisition round and the computer instrumentation pod on its pylons.

thus does not reveal that he had been singled for special attention.

JTIDS — Joint Tactical Information Distribution System — would have been termed pure fantasy a few years ago. This secure data link provides the Tornado's navigator with the same information as is available on the ground, covering all known sea and air deployments throughout the NATO area, constantly updated. Data is presented on a TV screen in the cockpit, the navigator selecting the small area in which the aircraft is currently operating. The principle is little different from the information systems available for domestic TVs, except that the Tornado will also contribute anything it finds to the overall picture.

Such will be the speed of combat that verbal communication is virtually to disappear. The data link will provide broad instructions from ground or an orbiting Boeing E-3A Sentry AWACS controlling the battle, and the Tornado's computer will work out the best tactics for combat: the order in which the enemy aircraft are to be attacked, and the optimum moment for missile release. For the RAF the 1990s will be the decade in which it will acquire the ability to conduct an air battle in radio silence without pilots once catching sight of the enemy.

Above:
As part of the defence in depth philosophy of NATO, Bloodhound plays an important role. Should any hostiles break through the airborne screen, Bloodhound forms the back-up area surface-to-air missile (SAM) force of the Royal Air Force.

Left:
A No 11 Group formation of Tornado F2, Phantom FG1, Lightning F3 and Hawk T1A represent the UK's air defence fighters of the 1980s.

Left and below:
Binbrook's Quick Reaction Alert (QRA) shed in the morning sun in late February 1982. At 10 min continuous readiness, QRA brings together the whole effort of RAF Binbrook and represents the station's main peacetime role. Credit must go to the engineers who must not only maintain the aircraft but keep the runway and taxiways clear of snow and ice in winter.

Right:
**An immaculate example
of a No 43 Squadron FG1
Phantom flown by former
Lightning pilot Sqn Ldr
John Cliffe.**

Far left and left:
A Phantom FGR2 of No 92 Squadron on alert in 'Battle' Flight, RAF Wildenrath, West Germany. The pilot's helmet is already connected into the aircraft radio and oxygen systems, thereby speeding up the reaction time.

Below:
The RAF UK Phantom force: an aircraft from each of Nos 64 (229 OCU), 29, 111, 43, 74 (black fin) and 56 Squadrons.

Above:
Chosen in preference to the Nimrod AEW3, the E-3 Sentry Airborne Warning & Control System (AWACS) will be entering RAF service in the early 1990s. The AWACS will give the extra 'over the radar horizon' view required by allied defences and enable early contact of hostiles. As a command post the E-3 will also correlate defence data and mission effectiveness.

Right:
Tornado ZD902 'AC' was delivered to No 229 OCU at Conningsby as the unit formed in 1985. This particular aircraft was one of six dual control aircraft, and with the gradual addition of 10 single-stick F2s the OCU's build-up was completed in October 1985.

Below:
No 229 OCU Tornados *en echelon*. Dual control ZD901 'AA' was one of the first two aircraft delivered to the OCU; ZD940 'AT' was one of the last F2s off the production line; and ZD905 'AV' served with the Aeroplane & Armament Experimental Establishment during the summer of 1985 before joining No 229.

Left:
Pilot Flt Lt Simon 'Much' Manning starts external checks whilst his navigator checks the cockpit.

Below:
Particular care is taken by Flt Lt Manning on his check of the live Sky Flash.

Bottom:
New aircraft entering service can pose large problems for engineers who need time to gain servicing experience. By the time Nos 29, 5 and 11 Squadrons form with the Tornado most of the lessons learnt by the OCU will have been passed on.

Right:
A Tornado F2 sits at RAF Valley in October 1986. In the foreground is a Sky Flash missile on its trolley.

Centre right and bottom right:
ZD932 'AM' is a Tornado F2 — note the short tailpipes of the RB199 Mk 103 fairing which cuts sharply away from the line of the rudder. The RAF's newer F3 has the improved Mk 104 engines, an extra two Sidewinder points achieved by activating the launch rail on the outboard of the pylons, and automatic wing sweep selection. Also clearly shown in this picture is the Operational Conversion Unit's torch-and-sword marking.

Below:
Tornado crew in the cockpit. The nose colours of No 229 OCU are now changing as the unit has been declared operational from the end of 1986, adopting the shadow wartime identity of No 65 Squadron. The new insignia is in the form of a lion passant and swords on a white disc, flanked by white bars with chevrons.

Top:
An early shot of British Aerospace, Warton's F2 ZA283 in September 1984.

Above:
An unlikely formation — who has the lead? The Jindivik Remotely Piloted Vehicle (RPV) had just completed its target towing run for the first in-service firing of Sky Flash, by ZD941, the last F2 built.

Left:
Grey air defence Hawks of Chivenor and Brawdy. Each of No 79, 234, 151 and 63 Squadrons are represented, and all have the capability for air-to-air and air-to-ground weapon delivery. The full armament inventory of the Hawk is commendable for what is primarily a trainer, but the most important of these weapons by RAF standards is the AIM-9 Sidewinder air-to-air missile.

Right:
Trainer with a potent sting — the Sidewinder-armed Hawk T1A, in air defence grey.

Below:
Pulling up or manoeuvring into the sun is a sometimes viable combat option. The difficulty is retaining 'tally' (visual contact with the enemy) whilst positioning for the kill.

Right:
A close-up of the Hawk's computer instrumentation pod which relays the carrier aircraft's speed, g loading, height and 'kill' position during combat engagements.

Above:
Cruising back to Decimomannu over the dry Sardinian backdrop. Well suited to overland operations, this grey-green camouflage on the Hawk can be a disadvantage in air-to-air engagements.

Top left:
Wingtip vortices give away the slight onset of 'g' during a three-ship pull-up.

Centre left:
Perhaps perfect formation? One each from the Binbrook Wing.

Below:
'Alpha Zulu' and 'Delta Bravo' of No 5 Squadron and the LTF. 'Delta Bravo' was being flown by Flt Lt I. McG. G. Howe (better known as K9) who at the time of writing was enjoying the luxury of an F-15 tour in the States. Unfortunately 'DB' no longer enjoys such scenery as it was lost in March 1987 during an aerobatic training sortie over Binbrook airfield. Fortunately, however, the pilot, Flt Lt Barry Lennon, survived a copy-book ejection.

Below:
Lightning F3 XP706 in quite an unusual and disorientating pose, pulling up before tipping in to the finals break on Binbrook's runway 03. The Binbrook engineering and domestic site lies to the south of the runway.

Bottom left:
Tools of the trade: 30mm rounds dipped with non-drying paint in a variety of colours. Aircraft are loaded with a specific colour which is then allotted to a particular pilot. Later the coloured holes in the banner are marked and scores awarded.

Above:
No 11 Squadron Armament Practice Camp, and Sqn Ldr Terry Adcock awaits the download of both Lightning Adens before being cleared to dismount following an air-to-air gunnery sortie.

Above left and left:
Cocking in a new belt of 30mm ammo, with the gun door removed to show more detail of the Aden mounting.

Left:
A two-seat 'tub', 'Alpha Zulu' of No 5 Squadron, RAF Binbrook.

Above:
Shadowing an air-to-air target banner.

Left:
Marking the target banner.

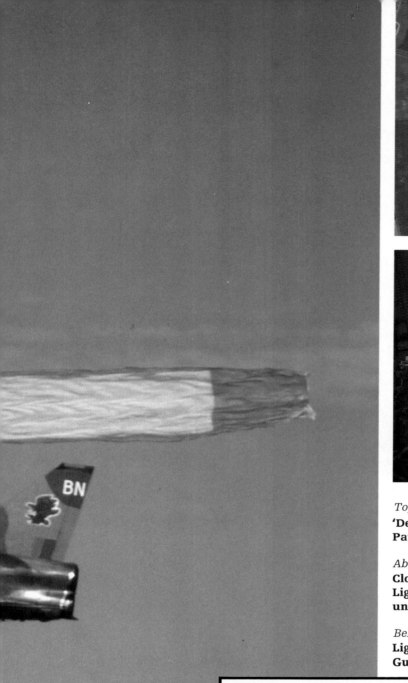

Top:
'Delta Foxtrot' XS923 of the LTF seen flown by Flt Lt Paul Field, now First Officer Field with British Airways.

Above:
Close-up of the cockpit and upper fuselage area of a T5 Lightning shot from a vertically-mounted camera hung under a Hawk.

Below:
Lightning F3s about to be pushed back into the Gutersloh 'Battle' Flight accommodation.

PER IGNEM VINCIMUS

THROUGH FIRE WE CONQUER

No 550 Squadron

Below:
A Dambusters' Tornado GR1 stands with CBLS 200 practice bomb carriers under the fuselage and 1,500-litre drop tanks on the inboard stations. This No 617 Squadron aircraft also shows the starboard muzzle of one of the two Mauser 27mm cannons (the ADV carries only one) and the 'clip-on' refuelling probe.

Bottom right:
No 17 Squadron Tornado GR1s bomb up for the Tactical Fighter Meet at Waddington in July 1986. In 1987 RAF Brüggen's No 17 was one of four ex-Jaguar squadrons equipped with Tornado, to be joined shortly by No 2 and another squadron operating dedicated reconnaissance Tornados.

At airfields all over blacked-out Lincolnshire, heavily-laden bombers struggled into the air, forming up by squadron and heading out over the North Sea. It seemed that the entire county was reverberating to the throbbing of Merlin engines as 560 Lancasters strained for altitude, weighed down by 1,795 tons of bombs destined for Hitler's Third Reich. Accompanying the deadly cargo were 3,920 young men, instructed in their diverse skills by a vast Empire Air Training Scheme, the outposts of which included Canada, South Africa and Australia. The following morning, Air Marshal Arthur Harris, C-in-C of Bomber Command, scanned the reconnaissance prints through half-moon spectacles, professing himself well-pleased with the result. Had one of his staff officers then prophesied that in years to come, 24 men in 12 aircraft called Tornados, carrying 48 tons of accurately-delivered bombs, would be able to achieve the same result, 'Bomber' Harris might well have had him locked up as insane.

Today, of course, pinpoint-delivery of conventional weaponry is fact, and a recent study has proved that 12 Tornados could have caused the same damage to the target (Peenemünde) as the raid cited above. Even during the flying training programme, students begin learning the skills necessary to achieve such economic results. Some members of the public may grumble when aircraft hurtle at low level along the sparsely-populated valleys of Scotland, Wales and the Lake District, but they are unaware that in a hostile air environment, low means comparatively safe. Such tactical skills are honed at the Tactical Weapons Units, where staff instructors flying Hawks lurk in wait for the student who is not taking full advantage of ground features in his mission planning. Those qualifying on the TWU's Offensive

Support course will find themselves posted to an OCU for the Tornado, Jaguar, Buccaneer or Harrier.

These are all strike and/or attack aircraft. The descriptions are often used imprecisely, yet have clear meanings in NATO parlance. Attack is, as might be supposed, an assault on an enemy facility, be it an airfield, ship, factory, storage dump, army unit or choke point (such as a river crossing), with *conventional* weapons. Strike is a similar mission using specifically *nuclear* weapons. Thus, most strike aircraft can undertake attack, but not all attack aircraft have a dedicated strike role. This is because some attack types have a lower standard of avionics and are optimised for short sorties to the battle front, not long and accurately-navigated forays well into enemy territory.

The BAe Harrier GR3, although no simple 'flying bomb trolley', falls into the attack-only category. Jaguars, Buccaneers and Tornados have increasing degrees of sophistication to enable them to undertake both roles. The Buccaneer is now assigned solely to maritime strike/attack from its last remaining base at Lossiemouth, Moray. Almost all the 65 surviving aircraft are Buccaneer S2Bs with the ability to launch Martel anti-ship missiles, No 237 OCU also having a few HS Hunter T7s for conversion training, as there are no dual control Buccaneers. All the aircraft allocated to Nos 12 and 208 Squadrons are undergoing a limited update for service well into the 1990s and are receiving Sea Eagle anti-ship missiles as a replacement for Martel.

Sea Eagle increases the aircraft's stand-off range three-fold to some 68 miles (110km) and is, in addition, a more 'intelligent', sea-skimming weapon. Other armament available to the Buccaneer includes the laser-guided bomb, which follows laser energy

Top left:
A Honington GR1 over the Wash.

Bottom left:
Nos 17 and 9 Squadron GR1s in full reheat launch as a pair.

Left:
Two No 31 Squadron aircraft depart in a reheat take-off, for a sortie during 1985's Exercise 'Mallet Blow'. The undercarriage retraction cycle is seen clearly.

Top:
Based at Brüggen, Tornado GR1 ZD843 'DH' of No 31 Squadron flies low over a snowy German landscape. The GR1's Command & Stability Augmentation System provides the crew with a more comfortable ride than on any other military aircraft optimised for low-level operations.

reflected from a target illuminated by a pod beneath the wing of an accompanying Buccaneer. Objectives for the Lossie strike wing are expected to be Soviet surface or amphibious groups either transiting the Iceland-Faroes Gap or attempting a landing in Norway.

Maritime combat missions require high standards of navigation over the featureless ocean and tend to be 95% routine and 5% mayhem. Little is encountered on the outward and return flights, but penetrating the destroyer screen and finding the highest-value target in the face of a barrage of anti-aircraft missiles more than compensates for the quiet periods. By contrast, the overland strike pilot earns his flying pay every inch of the way.

Apart from the threat of being 'bounced' by enemy fighters in the crowded air of Central Europe, a penetration mission carries with it the danger of overflying a SAM or gun position, which can be far better hidden than a ship on the ocean. Constant changes of course, complicating navigation, are thus necessary to avoid known danger areas. In fact it is not at all improbable that strike aircraft will have to fight it out with the defenders in order to reach their targets.

Recent changes and additions of equipment in the Anglo-French SEPECAT Jaguar are a clear example of the current trend. Once the principal strike/attack weapon of the RAF's forward force in Germany, the Jaguar is now flown on such missions only by UK

squadrons, and of 200 delivered (including 35 two-seat trainers), several have been retired or placed in storage. Unlike the Buccaneer and Tornado, the Jaguar is a non-radar aircraft, so lacking true all-weather operating capability. It is a single-seater, which imposes a high workload on the pilot, although it is fitted with a moving map display in the cockpit to ease the navigation task. Work has now been completed on updating Jaguars to GR Mk 1A standard with a more accurate inertial navigation system, and providing belly-mounted dispensers which eject SAM-confusing projectiles: if a heat-seeking SAM, a flare is dropped; if radar-guided, the Jaguar lays a cloud of metallic needles.

Optional equipment under the wings includes either a pair of AIM-9L Sidewinder air-to-air missiles for protection against fighters, or single examples of a radar-jamming pod and another type of flare dispenser. Such equipment is now standard with Nos 6, 41 and 54 Squadrons at Coltishall and No 2 at Laarbruch, Germany. Both No 2 and 41 Squadrons are tasked with tactical reconnaissance, for which their aircraft carry a 1,200lb (544kg) sensor pod under the fuselage. This contains conventional cameras as well as a linescan unit which takes 'heat' pictures in the infra-red spectrum, enabling it to see through foliage or camouflage netting to objects beneath.

Top:
Buccaneer on turnround — the unmistakable refuelling probe stands aloof above the F34 bowser. Some Buccaneers also have a tanker capability which, using the buddy-buddy technique, extends the tactical range of formations.

Above:
Flt Lt Tony Burtenshaw (Pilot) and Clive Lambourne taxi in following the Buccaneer display at RNAS Yeovilton in September 1986.

Left:
Royal Navy influence is still displayed as No 208 Squadron's Buccaneer S2B XX889 folds its wings whilst taxying in. With No 12 Squadron, No 208 provides the RAF's maritime attack capability and makes an important contribution to NATO in this role. They are backed up by an Operational Conversion Unit, No 237.

Top:
A No 208 Squadron Buccaneer descends to low level over the North Sea prior to engagements against No 11 Group air defence aircraft. Very stable at ultra-low level, the 'Bucc' is certainly no easy target and is particularly difficult to 'kill' with the gun.

Above:
A Buccaneer S2 of No 237 OCU RAF Lossiemouth, Scotland, flies high over the clouds. Unrefuelled, the Buccaneer has a typical sortie radius of 600 nautical miles.

Top and bottom right:
No 41 Squadron's Jaguars are tasked with tactical reconnaissance, utilising a centreline sensor pod. XZ114 'B' had this pod underslung when seen in 1987.

Far right, inset
The head up display (HUD) was brought into service to allow maximum 'head out' control by pilots, particularly for low-level operations. Here is the Jaguar display which provides altitude, speed, heading and height information to the pilot. Sophisticated air-to-air fighter aircraft also employ HUDs with air-to-air sighting and all-weather capabilities.

Even after conversion to Jaguars, a new recce pilot requires up to a year in the role before he can be considered proficient. Principally this is because of the demanding nature of the task, not least the fact that a sortie may involve overflying many targets, instead of attacking just one and returning to base. It can also be a hazardous duty if following a raid for damage assessment, as the defenders will be alert and more than a little irate. Then there are the area searches, which have to be carefully planned so as not to follow a predictable course when criss-crossing, yet covering every square yard of the designated zone.

Delivery of recce-configured Tornado GR1s to No 2 Squadron in 1988 will complete re-equipment of RAF Germany's strike/attack/recce force, complementing seven squadrons each equipped with some 13 of these aircraft from 1983 onwards. Nos 9, 14, 17 and 31 Squadrons are stationed at Brüggen, and Nos 15, 16

Top and above:
Low down over Scotland is No 226 OCU Jaguar T2 XX832 'S' from RAF Lossiemouth.

Left:
This rear-seat view of a Jaguar T2 shows the rear view mirror adjusted to pick up potential aggressors.

and 20 at Laarbruch, leaving just Nos 27 and 617 'The Dam Busters' in the UK, at Marham, Norfolk. By late 1985, when deliveries were temporarily halted, the RAF had received almost 200 of the 229 GR1s on order, some serving the Trinational Tornado Training establishment at Cottesmore, Leics, and the Tornado Weapons Conversion Unit at Honington, Suffolk ('shadow' No 45 Squadron).

Perhaps the most remarkable of the Tornado's many attributes is the ability to fly itself over the terrain at levels as low as 200ft (61m) entirely automatically in any weather. It is not without trepidation that pilot and navigator initially entrust their lives to a black box which will carry them over hill and dale, even avoiding power cables, but once confidence is gained they become part of a winning combination. Nose radar, an inertial navigation system and good management by the back seat occupant mean that the Tornado can fly for an hour out of visual contact with land and be at worst a mere 60ft (18m) from where the crew throught they were. With such phenomenal accuracy it is possible to guarantee a first-pass attack on any target in range — if necessary using a nearby prominent feature as an offset reference when the target is not visible.

Tornado weapons include nuclear devices as well as conventional ordnance, such as eight high explosive bombs of 1,000lb (454kg) each under the belly and the two internal 27mm Mauser cannon. If tasked against an airfield, the aircraft might use the JP233 dispenser which scatters 30 runway-cratering bomblets and, as an added bonus, 215 area-denial mines with several types of fuse (contact, delayed-action) to dampen the enthusiasm of repair parties. Against battlefield targets, the main weapon is Improved BL755, another cluster weapon, but this time one optimised for incapacitating vehicles.

If possible, NATO will restrict the Tornado to counter-air and interdiction roles, that is to say, striking at airfields and supply lines behind the battle area. It is the BAe Harrier which is supreme in the close support of troops, and again requires a different form of approach by pilots. In Germany, Nos 3 and 4 Squadrons operate the type from Gütersloh, whilst No 1 Squadron and No 233 OCU are the UK-based units at Wittering, Cambs. (A handful are stationed in Belize, Central America, with No 1417 Flight.) Nearly 70 of the 118 Harrier GR3s received since 1969, and over 20 of 27 T4/4A two-seat trainers, remain in service.

The Harrier's remarkable vertical take-off capability makes it unique on NATO's Central Front, for with the first sign of hostilities, the aircraft at Gütersloh will leave their base and take up position in six dispersed sites. To make them as difficult as possible to find, locations would be chosen such as a car park or motorway service station, offering a paved strip some 425ft (130m) long and — if possible

— some form of covered accommodation. This is because the Harrier is unable to take off vertically with a full load of fuel and weapons, and requires a short run if loaded with (say) three 1,000lb (454kg) bombs or BL755 cluster bombs in addition to its two belly-mounted 30mm cannon. Those of No 4 Squadron may also be fitted with a reconnaissance pod.

Even after allowance for the obvious disparities, Harrier flying is different from other forms of attack operation. Training has to be more intensive (there are, for example, six basic types of landing, not just one) and is prefixed by a short course of helicopter flying so that the pilot can overcome the inbuilt and very real fixed-wing flier's aversion to stopping an aeroplane in mid-air. On operations, the pilot will be required to fly more often than his compatriots assigned to other aircraft. Simply, this is the result of the Harrier forward operating locations being only 10-60 miles (16-96km) behind the forward line of NATO troops, considerably shortening the transit time from base to battle.

Put another way, the Harrier can respond with considerable speed to an urgent request for firepower. It is often the case on exercises that pilots will remain in their cockpits after landing whilst receiving their briefing for the next mission via a land-line plugged into the aircraft. When hardworking ground crew have re-armed the aircraft and refuelled it from large rubber 'pillow tanks' hidden under trees or in buildings, it will immediately taxi out from cover to the short runway. On return from the mission, the aircraft will be lighter and so can land vertically. Operating at this high intensity, each Harrier is able to generate 10 sorties in a five-hour period, compared with half that number for a Tornado based in the far west of Germany.

Top left:
**The Army Ground Liaison
Officer (GLO) briefs the
detachment on the
disposition of troops and
'enemy' targets in a No 4
Squadron Harrier field
deployment in 1985. From
this mobile HQ the tasking
orders can be passed on to
the pilots in the cockpit
and the mission results
passed back to overall HQ.**

Centre left:
**A Harrier pilot comes to
cockpit readiness. His
helmet will be connected
to the aircraft systems.**

Bottom and far left bottom:
**With the prospect of
chemical warfare, pilots
need protection from its
effects. Security comes in
the form of the AR5 all-in-
one respirator compatible
with current aviation
equipment.**

Right:
**The work room of the
Harrier.**

Below:
**Coming into the hide, a
No 3 Squadron Harrier
GR3 descends on to its
matted strip in a forest
clearing.**

Above:
Low level. The Harrier's role is mainly in support of ground forces at the heart of the action. Training missions involve the practising of these skills against simulated ground targets while keeping an eye out for 'enemy' fighters.

Right:
The view from the rear seat of a Harrier T4 about to 'pickle' (drop) a bomb on the Allham range in Germany.

Far right:
No 3 Squadron Harrier GR3s outside the squadron accommodation at Gütersloh, West Germany. In the background can be seen an open Hardened Aircraft Shelter (HAS).

Above:
A No 233 OCU Harrier T4 at Wittering. Early two-seaters were designated T2, but with the retrofitting of the 21,500lb thrust Pegasus 103 engine, they became T4s. These aircraft now also incorporate a radar warning receiver to indicate illumination by enemy radar.

Right and top centre:
Replacing a 30mm Aden cannon on a No 4 Squadron GR3 at Decimomannu.

Far right, top:
Soaking in the Sardinian sun, a No 4 Squadron GR3 awaits loading with practice bombs and 30mm rounds. The green umbrella is used to reduce cockpit temperatures prior to the pilot climbing in.

Far right, bottom:
Junior Technician Eastoe loads up a belt of 30mm rounds into one of the Harrier's Aden cannons.

Soon a new Harrier will be replacing its namesake in the skies of Britain and Germany. Resulting from American development of the basic airframe and engine, the considerably modernised and partly re-designed Harrier GR5 carries twice the payload of the earlier aircraft — up to 9,200lb (4,173kg) on short sorties. By the early 1990s, it will be capable of undertaking attack missions at night, with the pilot relying upon a forward-looking infra-red TV picture of the ground ahead projected on to a screen in his direct line of vision. It is invariably the way that what was regarded as science fiction when a pilot began his flying career is commonplace before it is completed.

Above and left:
When current fast-jet pilot training costs are running at £3 million it is not surprising that the Royal Air Force goes to great lengths to train pilots survival in all conditions likely to be encountered. Here Flt Lt Neil MachLachlan has been 'thrown' into the North Sea to fend for himself: his priorities are inflation of the Life Saving Jacket (LSJ) and single-man liferaft. Other survival courses within the service include training in snow-covered Bavaria and the jungles of Borneo.

The efforts of the RAF's Search and Rescue helicopters has saved numerous lives. XR507 is a Wessex HC2 of No 22 Squadron's 'D' Flight based at RAF Leconfield.

Whatever the type of aircraft he flies, the RAF pilot must be prepared for emergencies and accidents in his daily routine — hence the need for survival training. Most regularly practised, at RAF Mountbatten, Devon, is sea drill, this involving the victim being dropped from the back of a motor launch to simulate ejection over the sea. Kept afloat by his air-filled life-jacket, the pilot must haul in the survival pack to which he is attached by a 10ft (3m) lanyard, and inflate the one-man dinghy. First priority once aboard is to inflate the floor preventing heat loss to the sea, and then bail out, the body action helping to prevent any further loss of precious heat.

More enjoyable — though no more warm — are courses in winter survival which include the benefit of being able to learn to ski. More immediate lessons feature making a tent out of a parachute (with the dinghy as a li-lo) and the 'dos' and 'don'ts' of sleeping overnight in a snow-hole. Definitely not for the squeamish is the art of living off the land, using simple methods and country knowledge to find or trap food. It transpires that not many pilots are able to turn their hand with ease to the poacher's art, and the instructors always seem to make fieldcraft look easier than it really is. If a peaceful future is to be assured, the RAF — in league with its companion services — must continue to provide deterrence of the highest and most credible standard. Much of the responsibility falls upon the shoulders of pilots, yet it must never be forgotten that many serving men and women who never leave the ground also have an important role to play in keeping the RAF flying and fighting. Pilots merely have the privilege of taking aloft aircraft designed, built and maintained by thousands of unseen hands.

As he progresses through his chosen career — perhaps on fast jets at first, then transferring to instructing and transport flying — the demands of his task ensure that the pilot never forgets the ultimate purpose of constant practice. Long before 'Per Ardua Ad Astra' was coined as the RAF's motto, the 4th century writer Vegetius penned a succinct job description for Britain's junior armed force: 'Qui desiderat pacem, praeparet bellum': 'Let him who desires peace prepare for war' is entirely appropriate for a Service perpetually at the peak of readiness.

Above and right:
The author on winter survival training in Bavaria. Note that the parachute is rigged as a double-layered two-man tepee for insulation, and the floor of branches and ferns is for added ground insulation. The orange bag is a cutaway life jacket, washed out and used as a water bag.

Meanwhile Flt Lt Mike Carter, ex-Harrier pilot and one of the Red Arrows, attempts to dry his flying gloves before he and Flt Lt Allan prepare the evening meal. Dinner comes in the shape of rabbit hanging on the tree, with a dash of curry powder, followed by a boiled sweet.

Fire fighters tackle a
training fire — waste F34
aviation fuel ignites a
scrap hulk. Priorities
would include minimising
further risk and saving
crew. Here the sequence
illustrates the
effectiveness of foam
smothering the fire.